To all believers,

I have had to privilege of knowing Andrew Scales for 12 years. He first came to me looking for a job as a home health aide; someone to give of himself to help others in need.

His calm, mild manner created an instant trust and admiration of this man. Always pleasant and always cheerful, whenever asked how he is, his answer is the same: "I'm enduring."

The kindness this man has bestowed upon others is not often seen. The compassionate care he offers everyone is genuine and comforting. I am certain that many lives have been extended beyond natural course due to this man's nurturing and love.

I witnessed this first hand when I asked Andrew to come into my parents' home to care for my ailing father ten years ago. He was the perfect caregiver, as he possesses many of the respectable qualities that my dear father had. His easy-going nature is steady; his patience, beyond virtuous. A true guardian angel to my father, that when my dear father passed, I asked Andrew if he would grant my family the honor of being a pallbearer at my father's funeral. This man always treated my father with dignity and respect. He treats everyone he meets the same way.

Whatever Andrew believes has made him a remarkable humanitarian. I, too, believe.

Norma Goodman
RN and Owner of Infinity Home Health Services

This Is the Last Time!

This Is the Last Time!

To the seven city (churches)
which are in Asia

Andrew J. Scales

WestBow
PRESS
A DIVISION OF THOMAS NELSON

WestBow Press books may be ordered through
booksellers or by contacting:

WestBow Press
A Division of Thomas Nelson
1663 Liberty Drive
Bloomington, IN 47403
www.westbowpress.com
1-(866) 928-1240

The Holy Bible, Oxford, Printed at the University Press, London: Oxford
University Press, Brevier Clarendon Refs. W.M. & L.L. India Paper

ISBN: 978-1-4497-2418-4 (e)
ISBN: 978-1-4497-2419-1 (sc)

Library of Congress Control Number: 2011914717

Printed in the United States of America

WestBow Press rev. date: 6/29/2012

Contents

What I received!

A book for the seven churches that are in Asia in the name of LORD GOD ALMIGHTY, JESUS CHRIST, thanking the only GRAND FATHER!

PREFACE

I have put together what the LORD GOD JESUS CHRIST ALMIGHTY is going to do and what JESUS has done. It is written, "Write to the seven churches that are in Asia."

GOD is true, "I set to my seal, because of the books I received" This book is to share with all GOD'S children. We all read the same books (GOD'S Word). I call on our GRAND FATHER and LORD GOD, JESUS CHRIST ALMIGHTY. I received my testimony to share with you. This is the last time. I received the holy words more than thirty years ago. I went to many places, and some told me to get out. The lodge I'm in told me not to come into the meetings for one year. Now the year is up, and they told me I can come back into the meetings. They voted me in as chaplain. Then they told me not to pray on my knees, so I left. I was on the radio for fifteen years. A man brought the station, so I paid for my spots. The spots would not open up at the time I was suppose to go on, so he just took my money. (He also charged me two times the amount I was paying before.) I also paid a US paper to put in the paper, "I'm running in the race for the prize in the holy book I received." Only one man wrote me back after reading that in the paper.

Who believes in the LORD'S holy Word? If I was to teach, I would teach, "Read for yourself," for all GOD'S children stand alone. I put together what has happened and what is going to happen. Do GOD'S children know that all the children run in GOD'S race? Does anyone teach that?

Read 1 Corinthians 9:24-26v. Well, I'm running, and when I win, I will share it with all LORD GOD'S children. Do you know what LORD GOD JESUS delights in? It is written in Jeremiah 9:24v. It is written that first the gospel must be published among all the nations (Mark 13:10v.). I have shown you the book I received (John 16:14v.). Read the Revelation of JESUS CHRIST. To all GOD'S children, you are my witness. To the seven churches that are in Asia, each city, all the LORD GOD'S children and masons.

I thank our GRAND FATHER for the books I received, and that I know that His only Son is my (our) FATHER, the LORD GOD JESUS CHRIST ALMIGHTY.

Thank you,
Andrew Jesse Scales

I received this from the only GRAND FATHER.

This is the Revelation of JESUS to the seven churches. My name is Andrew Jesse Scales.

In the name of JESUS, I thank the only GRAND FATHER always. I am running in the LORD GOD JESUS' race. I am writing to the seven churches that are in Asia so what is written may be fulfilled. (Read Proverbs 1:7v.) Do GOD'S children despise wisdom and instruction? Fear of the only creator, the LORD GOD JESUS CHRIST ALMIGHTY, my FATHER and the only GRAND FATHER is my duty. We all read the same thing. (What are things to hope for? Faith?) (Read Job 13:2v.) I am not inferior to you. I am running in GOD'S race to win. I will share the prize with all GOD'S children. Will the children of GOD'S unbelief make the faith of GOD without effect? (Read Romans 3:3v.)

I can only write what was given me, and please don't take my words by themselves. Read for yourself. You stand alone!

More than thirty years ago I received these books, the Word, and I want to share them with all GOD'S children. This is my testimony unto the only GRAND FATHER (Rev. 19:10v.). The testimony of JESUS is the spirit of the prophecy. JESUS will show you better than I can read to you or you can read to yourself. Thank you for letting me read to you about what has happened and what is going to happen so I can run in the race that is set before me so I can be made free and you can too. These words are written to all my brothers and sisters. JESUS knows everything, and this is the last time. This book is for all GOD'S children (everyone), not just the seven churches that are in Asia. The Masonic orders that have not done their work, this book is mainly to you all. Remember, the time is at hand. We know the gospel must first be published among all nations. (Read Mark 13:10v.)

I am a brother. To all GOD'S children in every nation, read for yourself. This is the last time!

Revelation: Church of Ephesus

Let the race begin:

This is from Revelation 2:1-6v. Read for yourself. I am that I am. I am hoping to endure and to overcome, to become LORD GOD'S son. I read and write to the seven churches that are in Asia. (Read Rev. 2:6v.) Oh Ephesus, my LORD GOD ALMIGHTY writes: He (JESUS) holds the seven stars in His right hand and walks in the midst of the seven golden candlesticks. (Read Isa. 12:4v.) All will say praise the LORD and declare His doing. They will make mention His name, which is, will be exalted. I give light to the knowledge of understanding of what is written. Let your light shine too.

LORD GOD ALMIGHTY also knows your works, labor, and patience and how you cannot bear those who say they are apostles (teachers) and are not and found them liars.

And you have borne and have patience, and for my LORD name's sake, you have labored and have not fainted.

Oh children in the city of Ephesus (and all masons), my FATHER JESUS has somewhat against you because you have left your first love. (Read John 15:12v.) The

1

greatest commandment is that you love one another as I have loved you. What have we done to one another? Do we make one another go astray? I've been places and knocked, Guess what happened?. I went to churches of all kinds and Masonic halls of all kinds. Guess what happened.? I will tell what happened to everyone's face.

Repent! Do the first works. I know that you have not fainted. I also know that you hate the deeds of the Necolaitanes. Tell them to fight me. All evil fights me! Whatever my FATHER hates, I do too. Now I will show you that I understand and testify to my GRAND FATHER. All seven churches will be my witnesses (all nations). The church is in all GOD'S children, and as I write, you will be my witnesses too! Now I write to you what I read. Look up and let the light shine.

I write this book to all GOD'S children so you will know that I am running in GOD'S race. I must endure and overcome. I know that the only apostles are the twelve who were with JESUS at that time when He walked on the earth. It is written they will judge, and whoever says he or she is an apostle now lies. I know also those who say they are prophets and have Prophets dream. It's written: He who received the word, let him speak faithfully in the LORD'S word (Jer. 23:28v.). My first work is to publish the gospel of JESUS CHRIST ALMIGHTY of what has happened and the Revelation of what the LORD is going to do. I will be his son, and the LORD will be my GOD. Fear is an excellent gift of GOD. Where will wisdom be found, and where is the place of understanding? I cry for this world. All I see is pain.

Who has knowledge? What has the LORD done? The former prophets have cried, saying, "Thus saith the LORD of hosts; turn you now from your evil ways and from your evil doings: but your daddies did not hear, nor hearken unto my LORD." Because of the lack of knowledge and because they rejected knowledge, my LORD, my FATHER, rejected them. This is the last time! Please don't let Him reject you. Look up and let the light shine. As a mason, this is my work. What is a mason's work?

What JESUS Knows!
I Am that I Am. Look Up Rev 2: 1-6v.

Here is the answer to the mystery of the seven stars that is in the right hand of my LORD GOD and the seven golden candlesticks that you read are the seven churches. My LORD GOD is Alpha and Omega, the first and the last, and what I received is the light. The light is the Word that became the true and living Word. And it is written, "Write in a book, and send it unto the seven churches that are in Asia." You are the first city, Ephesus. Do not take my word for it. Read for yourself. If I could teach, I would teach you to read. You stand alone. GOD is not the author of confusion. You can read about the other six churches in this book.

My (our) FATHER LORD GOD JESUS CHRIST ALMIGHTY has in His right hand seven stars, and out of his mouth went a sharp, two-edged sword. His countenance was as the sun shining in his strength. And in the mist of the seven candlesticks was one like the Son of Man who clothed with a garment down to His feet and girded with a golden girdle. Also to the wise, judge in yourselves: is it comely that a woman pray unto GOD uncovered? Remember the Word of the LORD that came in the days of Josiah, the son of Amon king of Judah, in the thirteenth year of his reign. It is written, "Even a child knows right from wrong." Remember that the words of the LORD are like fire. In the latter days all GOD'S children will consider it. The masons all took a vow. The LORD will pay them to their faces. Is not the church in each child of GOD?

Left First Love! To the Wise

To the wise, who understand? (John 21:22v.) "JESUS saith unto him, if I will that he tarry till I come, what is that to you? Follow you me." I cannot go away. I call on my LORD. Do you children want me to go away? Where can I go but to the LORD and my GRAND FATHER? I am so happy that I have two, and me and my brothers and sisters make three. I am a sinner and come short of glory. Who are you who judges? Is it not written judge yourself first? To the wise, my FATHER LORD will miserably destroy those wicked men and will let out His vineyard to other husbandmen who will render Him the fruits in their seasons. Therefore say I unto you the kingdom of GOD will be taken from you, and given to a nation bringing forth the fruits thereof. Please do not let your vineyard be taken away. Now is the time to do what you vow.

Remember what is written unto you. It is written,(Revelation 2:1v.) "Unto the angel of the church of Ephesus write: These things said he that hold the seven stars in his right hand, who walketh in the mist of the seven golden candlesticks." The LORD GOD is in the midst of all the children.

Do you want to know what our GOD looks like? It is written, (Revelation 2;15v.) "His feet are like unto fine brass, as if they burned in a furnace; and his voice as the sound of many waters."

Look up why? To the wise,(Act 6:5v.) "Ananias, hearing these words, fell down and gave up the ghost: and great fear came on all them that heard these things." He who has an ear, let him hear. Repent!

Oh my brothers and sisters, fear the LORD GOD. This is the last time.

Revelation: Church of Smyrna

Let the race begin!

Read Revelation 2:8-10v.

I am that I am. I hope to endure, to overcome, and to become LORD GOD'S son. These words are written unto the second church, Smyrna. I write,(Revelation 2:8&9v.) "These things, saith the first and the last, which was dead, and is alive; I know thy works, and tribulation, and poverty, (but you are rich) and I know the blasphemy of them which say they are Jew, and are not, but are the synagogue of Satan. O children in the city of Smyrna!" This also applies to all masons. I have read,(Revelation 2:10v.) "Fear none of those things which you shall suffer: I am the runner, that will endure with you, for you shall have tribulation ten days: be you faithful unto death, and My FATHER will give you a crown of life." All Jews are not Jews. Our faith makes all GOD'S children strong, thanking our GRAND FATHER. I write to all GOD'S children like they have not read or heard that the LORD is the truth, for our faith is the substance we hope for. Our faith makes us rich in hoping for that which we cannot see. We know that the LORD breathed into man, and our faith is the breath we breath. All my brothers and sisters, be strong in the LORD and your expectation shall not be cut off.

It is written in Proverbs 23:17v., "For surely there is an end; and thine expectation shall not be cut off, for I set to my seal that GOD *is true."* Our GRAND FATHER, the Son, the LORD GOD will avenge us (Luke 21:22v.). It is for these be the days of vengeance that all things that are written may be fulfilled. Will see you before these things happen. These words are written to you. (St. Mark 13:10v.). "We know that first the gospel has to be published among all nations." Now look up from where (our) your help comes. The time is closer than you think! We will endure together by reading and learning what has happened and what is going to happen. What do we know about the LORD GOD? Why do the children not want to talk about GOD'S Word?

What JESUS Knows!
I Am That I Am. Look Up Rev. 2: 8-10v.

If you believe not GOD'S writings, how will you believe my word? I am poor too, and I cry out to the Alpha and Omega, the first and the last. Running, I write and put words in a book for all the LORD GOD'S children. I thank our GRAND FATHER for the love of LORD GOD JESUS CHRIST ALMIGHTY that the GRAND FATHER has given us. Be strong and hold on. These words are written to the city Smyrna (and all masons).

It is written: (Revelation 1:18v.) "My FATHER that liveth, and was dead; and, behold, is alive for evermore, Amen." The LORD has the keys of hell and of death. Hearken, my beloved brethren (and sisters). Hath not GOD chosen the poor of this world to be rich in faith and heirs of the kingdom He has promised to those who love Him? You are called a Jew and rest in a law and make your boast of GOD. I too make boast of the LORD GOD (John 8:32v.). We will know the truth, and the truth will make us free. I love our LORD GOD FATHER, for JESUS is love! In the United States the Jews I know say my GRAND FATHER is their GOD. Most masons say JESUS is our brother. Who has been teaching us? I read that he who believes on the Son of GOD has the witness in himself. He who believes not GOD has made him a liar because he believed not the record GOD gave of His Son (1 John 5:10v.).

My LORD GOD will make them of the synagogue of Satan who say they are Jews and are not but do lie. Behold, my FATHER LORD GOD will make them to come and worship before your feet and to know that my LORD has loved us. My LORD GOD knows your works and where you dwell, even where Satan's seat is. You hold fast GOD'S name and have not denied the faith, even in those days when Antipas was the LORD'S faithful martyr who was slain among you where Satan dwells. But unto you my LORD says and unto the rest in Thyatira as many as have not this doctrine (of Satan) and who have not known the depths of Satan, as they speak, my LORD will put upon you no other burden. I hope the Jews know this is the truth. Who has been tricking my brothers and sisters?

Behold, you are called a Jew and rest in a law and make your boast of GOD. I will know the difference between my brother Jew and the ones who call themselves Jews and do lie.

Our LORD GOD wrote, (Revelation 3:9v.) "Behold, I will make them of the synagogue of Satan, which say they are Jews, and are not, but do lie; behold, I will make them to come and worship before thy feet, and to know that I have loved you." This is to the wise: when they come, what will they say?

My FATHER and I know your works and where you dwell, even where Satan's seat is. You hold fast to my LORD GOD'S name and have not denied my faith, even in those days when Antipas was my LORD'S faithful martyr, who was slain among you, where Satan dwells.

But unto you and unto the rest in Thyatira I say as many as have not this doctrine, and which have not known the depths of Satan, as they speak, my LORD will put upon you no other burden. All those who are against my FATHER LORD GOD and my GRAND FATHER, I will fight them with the sword that is in my mouth. Our LORD GOD'S Word is as a fire and like a hammer that breaks the rock in pieces (Jer. 23:29v.).

Old Serpent!

Remember what our FATHER LORD GOD will make of them of the synagogue of Satan who say they are Jews and are not but do lie. Behold, our FATHER will make them come and worship before your feet and to know that the LORD GOD has loved us.

I must be about my work that I received. This will happen so the great dragon will be cast out, that old serpent called the devil and Satan who deceives the whole world. He was cast out into the earth, and his angels were cast out with him. They say this already happened, and they lie. Do you remember the woe unto the earth, for the devil has come down and has but a short time?

He laid hold on the dragon, that old serpent, which is the devil, and Satan, and bound him a thousand years. A thousand years are only a day to my FATHER LORD GOD.

And when the thousand years are expired, Satan will be loosed out of his prison. Have you read one day is as a thousand years to our GOD? To the wise, deliver such a one unto Satan for the destruction of the flesh, that the spirit may be saved in the day of the LORD JESUS.

My LORD has said these things have been written to you that in the LORD GOD you might have peace. In the world you will have tribulation, but be of good cheer—my

LORD has overcome the world. I, Andrew Jesse Scales, will endure and will overcome too, and all GOD'S children will be with me and my FATHER.

To the wise: "And her brother and her mother said, Let the damsel abide with us a few days, at the least ten; after that she shall go, come, come."

But CHRIST Has a Son!

I will come unto you, for I too am a servant. Prove your servants, I beseech you, for ten days, and let them give us plulse to eat and water to drink.

Will my brothers and sisters please consent to them in this matter and proved them ten days?

I too will be hated, and you will be hated by all men for my LORD name's sake. But he who endures to the end will be saved.

I read CHRIST as a son (I hope to be) over His own house, whose house you are if you hold fast to the confidence and the rejoicing of the hope firm unto the end.

I too know your works and where you dwell, even where Satan's seat is, and you hold fast my FATHER's name and have not denied our faith, even in those days when Antipas was my LORD'S faithful martyr, who was slain among you, where Satan dwells.

These will make war with the Lamb, and the Lamb will overcome them, for he is the LORD of LORDs and King of kings. Those who are with him are called and chosen and faithful.

Moreover, it is required in stewards that a man be found faithful.

Blessed is the man who endures temptation, for when he is tried, he will receive the crown of life, which the LORD hath promised to those who love Him. He who has ears, let him hear.

Oh Smyrna, fear our LORD, who have the keys of hell! I hope to see you. This is the last time.

John 16:33v.: "These things I have spoken unto you, that in me ye might have peace. In the world ye shall have tribulation: but be of good cheer: I have overcome the world."

Revelation: Church of Pergamum

Third Church: Pergamos

Revelation 2:12-16v.

These words are written: (Revelation 2:12v.) "I write unto the churches in the city of Pergamos write [also all mason lodges]; these things saith he which hath the sharp sword with two edges." Also let the words from my mouth be my sword. My GOD will get this world. My LORD GOD ALMIGHTY will have His vengeance!

I too, the son of CHRIST, know your works and where you dwell, even where Satan's seat is. You hold fast my FATHER's name and have not denied my LORD faith, I read, even in those days when Antipas was my LORD'S faithful martyr, who was slain among you where Satan dwells.

I too, as my LORD GOD, have a few things against you, because you have there those who hold the doctrine of Balaam, who taught Balac to cast a stumbling block before the children of Israel, to eat things sacrificed unto idols, and to commit fornication (Num. 31:16v.).

You also have those who hold the doctrine of the Nicolaitanes, which I hate as my FATHER (the LORD) hates.

Repent or else I will come unto you quickly and will fight against them with the sword of my mouth. I set to my seal that GOD is true! The LORD'S Word is like fire. Have you not read?

What JESUS Knows!
I Am that I Am! Look Up Rev. 2:12-16v.

Have you read the mystery of the seven stars that you saw in the LORD GOD right hand and the seven golden candlesticks? The seven stars are the angels of the seven churches and the seven candlesticks.

It is written I should say and write unto you,(Revelation 1:11v.) "My LORD GOD is, Alpha and Omega, the first and the last: and, What I have seen, I write in a book, and I will send it unto the seven churches which are in Asia; unto Ephesus, and unto Smyrna, and unto Pergamos, and unto Thyatira, and unto Sardis, and unto Philadelphia, and unto Laodicea."

Repent or else I will come to you quickly and will fight against them with the sword of my mouth. Repent.

And my FATHER had in His right hand seven stars, and out of His mouth went a sharp, two-edged sword. His countenance was as the sun shining in his strength. Who shall not fear my GOD (Rev. 1:16v.)!

The book I will show you is for edification. I have read. I too know your works, tribulation, and poverty (but you are rich), and I know the blasphemy of those who say they are Jews and are not but are the synagogue of Satan.

Have you not read, I Timothy 5:8v., "If any provide not for his own, and specially for those of his own house, he hath denied the faith, and is worse than an infidel." None of GOD'S houses do their duty. at the lodge I was in and still am in a man called me a infidel. I went and looked it up. I told him it was not over until I said so. Before the LORD laid him to rest, he asked me to leave him alone. (He told me he was sorry. Ha!)

"For I am doing the will of GOD, that with well doing I will put to silence the ignorance of foolish men and women" (2 Peter 2:15v.).

I am a mason. The light I received is to share with all GOD'S children. I will proclaim the acceptable year of the LORD and the day of vengeance of our GOD. Oh children of GOD, comfort all who mourn (Isa. 61:2v.).

That Woman Jezebel

As it is written like my GOD, notwithstanding the LORD has a few things against you, because you suffer that woman Jezebel, who calls herself a prophetess, to teach and to seduce my servants to commit fornication and to eat things sacrificed unto idols. Repent! In every city in the world, do they have a prophetess?

You need to abstain from meats offered to idols, from blood, from things strangled, and from fornication. If you keep yourselves from these, you will do well. Fairly well. Stop letting the Jezebels of this world trick you (Acts 15:29v.).

My LORD GOD gave Jezebel space to repent of her fornication, and she repented not (Reve. 2:20v.).

Have you read that Israel abode in Shittim, and the people began to commit whoredom with the daughters of Moab (Num. 25:1v.)?

Behold, these caused the children of Israel, through the counsel of Balaam, to commit trespass against the LORD in the matter of Peor, and there was a plague among the congregation of the LORD. Oh children, how long will it be before the day comes when Balaam will be no more (Num. 31:16v.)?

Have you read, 1 Corinthians 10:8v., "Neither let us commit fornication, as some of them committed, and fell in one day three and twenty thousand" (1 Cor. 10:8v.)?

I read, Revelation 2:6v., This you have, that you hatest the deeds of the Nicolaitanes, which my FATHER also hate."

Have you read what is going to happen to Jezebel? They are going to eat her and kill her children? Ha! Who will not fear our LORD GOD ALMIGHTY?

The Wicked Will Be Revealed!

As I write to all the children, my FATHER has in His right hand seven stars, and out of his mouth went a sharp, two-edged sword. His countenance was like the sun shining in his strength (Rev. 1:16v.).

I will with righteousness judge the poor and reprove with equity the meek of the earth. The LORD will let me smite the earth with the rod of my mouth, and with the breath of my lips will I slay the wicked (Isa. 11:4v.).

And then will the wicked be revealed who the LORD will consume with the spirit of His mouth and destroy with the brightness of His coming. He who has an ear, let him hear (2 Thess. 2:8v.).

I will glorify my LORD GOD, for I will show everyone what I received (John 16:14v.).

Fear! All will fear our LORD GOD and will testify to our GRAND FATHER! My brothers and sisters do well, for I will come, come, come.

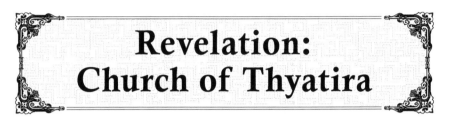

Revelation:
Church of Thyatira

Fourth Church: Thyatira

Revelation 2:8-25v.

I write these words to the city in Thyatira (and all mason lodges around the world). These things say the Son of GOD (the only FATHER) who has eyes like a flame of fire, and his feet are like fine brass. Who is like our GOD?

My FATHER and I know your works, charity, service, faith, patience, and works, and the last will be more than the first. Have you read first what will be last?

Notwithstanding, I and my FATHER have a few things against you, because you suffer that woman Jezebel, who calls herself a prophetess, to teach and to seduce my servants to commit fornication and eat things sacrificed to idols.

My LORD GOD gave Jezebel space to repent of fornication, and she repented not. Have you not read what has happened and what is going to happen?

My GOD will cast her into a bed and those who commit adultery with her into a great tribulation unless they repent of their deeds.

And I will kill her children with death. All the (children) churches will know that the LORD is He who searches the minds and hearts, and my LORD will give unto every one of you according to your works. Who will not fear our LORD?

But unto you it is written, "Unto the rest in Thyatira, as many as have not this doctrine, and which have not known the depths of Satan, as they speak; my LORD GOD will put upon you none other burden."

But what you have already hold fast until I come. I am that I am to give the testimony about all my brothers and sisters. We all come short of the glory of GOD. The LORD, that everlasting GOD, the LORD, the creator of the ends of the earth, faints not, and neither is He weary. Have you not heard? Have you not known (Isa. 40:28v.).

What JESUS Knows!
I Am that I Am! Look Up.

Remember what I write unto you I say, and to the rest in Thyatira, as many as have not this doctrine, and who have not known the depths of Satan as they speak. My LORD will put upon you no other burden.

My LORD GOD is the Alpha and Omega, the first and the last. What you see I now write in a book and send unto the seven churches that are in Asia: unto Ephesus, and unto Smyrna, and unto Pergamos, and unto Thyatira, and unto Sardis, and unto Philadelphia, and unto Laodicea (Rev. 1:11v.).

You want to know how LORD GOD looks. It is written that His head and His hairs were white like wool, as white as snow, and His eyes were as a flame of fire. (Read it in Revelation 1:14v.).

To the wise, do you remember reading that it came to pass, as if it was a light thing for him to walk in the sins of Jeroboam the son of Nebat that he took to wife Jezebel the daughter of Ethbaal, king of the Zidonians, and went and served Baal and worshipped him (1 Kings 16:31v.).

Oh children! But there was none like unto Ahab, who sold himself to work wickedness in the sight of the LORD, whom Jezebel his wife stirred up (1 Kings 21:25v.).

To the wise, read 2 Kings 9:7v. "And soon you shalt smite the house of Ahab thy master, that I may avenge the blood of my servants the prophets and the blood of all the servants of the LORD, at the hand of Jezebel." Why have my brothers and sisters not read that our LORD GOD does not forget? The days of vengeance will come to pass, so that all things that are written may be fulfilled. Have you not read that when I overcome, JESUS my FATHER will sit me in His seat, just like my FATHER overcame and my GRAND FATHER set him in the throne (Rev. 3:21v.).

Concerning His Promise!

This is going to happen (Rev. 9:20-21v.). During the days of vengeance, the seal was open, the horns was blow, and the rest of the men who were not killed by these plagues did not repent of the words of their hands, that they should not worship devils and idols of gold, silver, brass, stone, and wood that neither can see nor hear nor walk. (Read about vengeance for the saints in Revelation 6:9v.)

They did not repent of their murders, sorceries, fornication, or thefts (Rev. 9:21v.).

"Because they despisest us the riches of my FATHER goodness and forbearance and long suffering; not knowing that the goodness of GOD leadeth you to repentance" (Rom. 2:4v.).

My LORD GOD is not slack concerning His promise as some men count slackness but is longsuffering to us. He is not willing that any should perish but that all should come to repentance. (Do you know where this is written?)

Oh, let the wickedness of the wicked come to an end but establish the just, for the righteous GOD tries the hearts and minds. Now by the Word it is published among all nations (Psalms 7:9v.). Repent, my brothers and sisters. All have come short of glory (Ps.1:22v.). Simple ones love simplicity, scorners delight in their scorning, and fools hate knowledge. Do you hate knowledge?

I will, and you can too, see the dead, small and great, stand before GOD; and the books will be opened and another book will be opened, the book of life. The dead will be judged out of those things that were written in the books according to their works (Reve 20: 12-13v.).

And the sea gave up the dead that were in it and death and hell delivered up the dead that were in them, and they were judged, every man according to his works. Oh children, I set to my seal that GOD is true!

Remember!

I also wrote to the city of Pergamos (all masons). My LORD GOD, who has the sharp sword with two edges knows you also. Oh my LORD GOD, to You belong mercy, for You render to every man according to his work (Ps 62:12v.).

For it is written, "As I live, saith the LORD, every knee shall bow to me, and every tongue shall confess to GOD. O children this is my testimony, this is the last time" (Rom.14:12v.; Isa.45:23v.; Phil.2:10v.).

I see your works, tribulation, and poverty (but you are rich), and I know the blasphemy of those who say they are Jews and are not but are the synagogue of Satan.

I know unto GOD are all His works from the beginning of the world.

Behold, I come quickly. Hold fast to what you have, so no man can take your crown (Rev. 3:11v.).

I will come to you first. Remember, therefore, how you received and heard, and hold fast, and repent. If therefore you will not watch, my FATHER LORD GOD will come on you as a thief, and you will not know what hour He will come upon you. Please, be strong overcome to the end. Oh GRAND FATHER, Your Son's will and Your's will be done (Rev. 3:3v.).

Oh Thyatira, Fear GOD! The time is at hand.

PS: It is written, "CHRIST has a son over his house" (to the wise, read Hebrews 3:6v.).

Revelation: Church of Sardis

Fifth Church: Sardis

Revelation 3:1-4v. Says, "I write unto the children in Sardis [also all the masons in every nation]; All GOD'S children you carry the church in you. (Rev. 5:10v.). These things saith LORD GOD ALMIGHTY that hath the seven Spirits of GOD, and the seven Stars; I know thy works, that you have a name that you livest, and art dead." (Revelation 3:1v.)

I read that you should be watchful and strengthen the things that remain (our brothers and sisters) that are ready to die. I read my LORD GOD has not found your works perfect before GOD. My LORD GOD knows your work. I have not seen a mason or a star strengthen anything, not even in the house of prayer. So remember, therefore, how you have received and heard, and hold fast and repent. If, therefore, you will not watch, I will come first, and my FATHER will come on you as a thief, and you will not know what hour my LORD will come upon you.

When I come, I will meet the few named even in Sardis that have not defiled their garment. They will walk with me in white, for they are worthy. Remember also I will come and you will see me, but you will not see our LORD GOD, the Creator of everything, when He comes as a thief.

What JESUS Knows.
I Am that I Am. Look Up 3:1-4v.

I will write on the wise to the city of the churches in Philadelphia (also the masons): These things says my LORD GOD who is holy and true, who has the key of David, who opens and no man shuts and no man opens. Who changed the Word of GOD into a lie and worshipped and served the creature more than the Creator (Rom. 1:25v.)?

I also will write on the wise to the city of Laodiceans (to all mason). These things says the amen, the faithful and true witness, the beginning of the creation of my GRAND FATHER GOD.

You two churches have a few names even in Sardis that have not defiled their garment, and they will walk with me in white, for they are worthy.

Remember, our LORD GOD is the Alpha and Omega, the first and the last: and, what I write is in a book as it is written. Publish a book and send it to the seven churches that are in Asia: unto Ephesus, and unto Smyrna, and unto Pergamos, and unto Thyatira, and unto Sardis, and unto Philadelphia, and unto Laodicea (Rev. 1:11v.).

John wrote to you, now I write and put it in a book. Grace be unto you and peace from Him who is and who was and who is to come and from the seven Spirits who are before his throne (Rev. 1:4v.). Do you know where it is written John will come again?

My LORD GOD has in His right hand seven stars, and out of his mouth went a sharp, two-edged sword, and his countenance was as the sun shining in his strength. I am running in a race. My LORD GOD, my FATHER, the ALMIGHTY, will this once cause everyone to know His hand and His might. The LORD is His name (Jer. 16:21v.).

My LORD GOD and I know your works, labor, and patience and how you cannot bear those who are evil, and you have tried them who say they are apostles (teachers) and are not and have found them liars. I know a truth: only JESUS has apostles.

Watch, Therefore!

Our LORD GOD will quicken those who were dead in trespasses and sins (Eph. 2:1v.).

All the churches will know when I come, but you will not know when our LORD comes, so watch, therefore, for you do not know at what hour your LORD will come (Matt. 24:42v.).

The LORD wants all the children to know (as it is written), "Behold, I come as a thief. Blessed is he that watcheth, and keepeth his garments, lest he walk naked, and they see his shame. All my brothers and sisters will received their white garments, so watch" (Rev. 16:15v.).

And know this, that if the goodman of the house had known in what watch the thief would come, he would not have let his house be broken up. Even if you close the house and quit your job, you will be found (Matt. 24:43v.).

I write you a truth: as many as I and my FATHER love, my FATHER will rebuke and chasten. Be zealous, therefore, and repent.

"But what you have already hold fast till I come." (Revelation 2:25v.)

When you see me, know what is written. "And the same hour was there a great earthquake, and tenth part of the city fell, and in the earthquake were slain of men seven thousand: and the remnant were affrighted, and gave glory to the GOD of heaven" (Rev. 11:13v.).

What will be in our days? In the days of Peter when he stood up in the midst of the disciples, he said the number of names together were about an 120 (Acts 1:15v.).

You are the ones who were not defiled with women, for you are virgins. These are those who follow the Lamb wherever he goes. These were redeemed from among men, being the first fruits unto GOD and to the Lamb (Rev. 14:4v.).

He Who Overcomes!

Are you still saving one another? "With fear, pulling them out of the fire; hating even the garment spotted by the flesh" (Jude v. 23v.).

I will also confess if you endure and overcome with me, you will be clothed in white raiment, and my LORD GOD will not blot your name out of the book of life. I will confess your name before my FATHER and before His angels.

I and my FATHER know your work. Behold, our FATHER has set before you an open door, and no man can shut it, for you have a little strength and have kept my word and have not denied my FATHER's name. Let us strengthen one another.

You and I will see our LORD GOD sitting on His throne and around the throne were four and twenty seats, and upon the seats I saw four and twenty elders sitting clothed in white raiment, and they had on their heads crowns of gold (Rev. 4:4v.).

To the wise, "Remember, keep in your mind, thy garment will be always white; and let thy head lack no ointment" (Eccles. 9:8v.).

"His countenance was like lightning, and his raiment white as snow: Him that overcometh will see and be in eternity (Matt. 28:3v.).

I say to all my brothers and sisters, "Fear GOD!" This is the last time! May our LORD GOD ALMIGHTY strengthen us.

Ps. Philemon 4:3v., "Grace to you, and peace, from GOD, our FATHER and the LORD JESUS CHRIST."

Revelation: Church of Philadelphia

Sixth Church: Philadelphia!

Revelation 3: 7-11v. "I write to the city in Philadelphia [and also mason's lodges]; These things saith my LORD GOD that is holy, he that is true, he that hath the key of David, he that openeth, and no man shutteth; and shutteth, and no man openeth [to the wise]. I know thy works and my FATHER does too: behold, FATHER has set before you an open door, and no man can shut it: for you have a little strength, and have kept the LORD'S word, and have not denied JESUS name."

Behold, My FATHER will make them of the synagogue of Satan, which says they are Jews and are not but lie. Behold, our LORD will make them come and worship before your feet and know that our LORD have loved you. Have you read, "JESUS is love?"

Because the children of Philadelphia have kept the word of my FATHER's patience, my FATHER also will keep you from hour of temptation, which shall come upon all the world to try those who dwell upon the earth.

Behold, my FATHER and I will come quickly. Hold fast to what you have so no man will take your crown.

Oh! children, once the truth is published, it will not take long before knowledge come all over this wold. Who will not fear our LORD GOD?

What JESUS Knows!
I Am that I Am! Look Up Revelation 3:7-11v.

I set to my seal that my FATHER is the Alpha and Omega, the first and last. What you see I have published in a book, and I will send it to the seven churches that are in Asia: unto Ephesus, and unto Smyrna, and unto Pergamos, and unto Thyatira, and unto Sardis, and unto Philadelphia, and unto Laodicea.

As it is written, my brothers are crying, saying, "How long, O LORD, holy and true, will you not judge and avenge our blood on those that dwell on the earth? Have you not read this? When will this be?" (Rev. 6:10v.). Do the brothers and sisters care about them?

And unto the city of Laodiceans I will write, "These things saith the amen, the faithful and true witness, the beginning of the creation of GOD. Laodiceans is the seventh city, there must be family there" (Rev. 3:14v.).

This is a truth, what John saw: "And I, John saw heaven opened, and behold a white horse; and he that sat upon him was called Faithful and True, and in righteousness he doth judge and make war" (Rev. 19:11v.).

We know that the Son of GOD is come and has given us understanding so we may know Him who is true, and we are in Him who is true, even in His Son JESUS CHRIST.

This is the true GOD and eternal life. Oh children, the truth is judgment that will come from the LORD (Prov. 29:26v.). I pray that the LORD will give wisdom to His children. We read, "The LORD gives wisdom: by reading we received knowledge and understanding" (Prov.2:6v.).

"And the key of the house of David will I lay upon his shoulder; so he shall open, and none shall shut; and he shall shut, and none shall open" (Isa. 22:22v.). We read that our GRAND FATHER put all power into His Son's hands. Oh children, when I win the race my FATHER, LORD GOD JESUS CHRIST ALMIGHTY, will make me his son. (If I overcome, it is written in Revelation and other places that the LORD will do and give me this.) My GRAND FATHER gave me the Word. He is our FATHER, and I will sit with them.

I want all GOD'S children to know, that I am running to be the son of LORD FATHER JESUS. THANK OUR GRAND FATHER!

Son of the Highest!

"He will be great and will be called the son of the Highest: and the LORD GOD shall give unto him the throne of his FATHER David" (Luke 1:32v.). Here is wisdom for me when I overcome.

I will give to you the keys of the kingdom of heaven, and whatever you bind on earth will be bound in heaven, and whatever you loose on earth will be loosed in heaven. Oh children, let justice go home. Where can we go but to the LORD?

I am that I am sent me, My FATHER who lives, and was dead, and behold, we read, "My FATHER is alive for evermore, amen; and have the keys of hell and of death" (Rev. 1:18v.).

"Behold, Our FATHER breaketh down, and it cannot be built again: he shutteth up a man, and there can be no opening" (Job 12:14v.).

When we come together, let me know, as it is written: "And when they were come, and had gathered into the church together, they rehearsed all that GOD had done with them, and how he had opened the door of faith unto the Gentiles" (Acts 14:27v.). I will also let you know what GOD has done for me so far and what He is going to do.

To the wise: "I know thy works, and tribulation, and poverty,(but you are rich) and I know the blasphemy of them which say they are Jews and are not, but are the synagogue of Satan" (Rev. 2:9v.).

Kings will be your nursing fathers and their queens your nursing mothers. They will bow down to you with their face toward the earth and lick up the dust of you feet. You will know I am the LORD, for they will not be ashamed who wait for me. I, Andrew Jesse Scales, am not ashamed of my LORD, and I will overcome. I will endure! (Read Isaiah 49:23v.) Remember, read for yourself.

Fear None!

Call on our LORD GOD, our FATHER, so He will do what is written and make the sons of those who afflicted you come bending to you. All those who despised you will bow themselves down at the soles of your feet, and they will call you the city of the LORD, the Zion of the Holy One of Israel (Isa. 60:14v.). Oh Philadelphia, what city is like unto you? I set to my seal that GOD is true (to the wise).

"Remember he that lacketh these things is blind, and cannot see afar off, and hath forgotten that he was purged from his old sins. O children you can see so there is no excuse, is there?" (2 Peter 2:9v.).

I will come when you read this, but, you will not know when the LORD GOD FATHER JESUS CHRIST ALMIGHTY will come. Behold, I come quickly. Blessed is he who keeps the sayings of the prophecy of this book. John fell to worship the angel that showed him these thing I write unto you. The angel told him that he too was a fellow servant: worship GOD! (See Rev. 22:7&12v.).

It is written, "JESUS saith unto him, If I will that he tarry till I come, what is that to you? follow you me." I say to you, follow "JESUS." Read for yourself." I need no one following me. I am running in a race (John 21:22v.).

To the wise and those not holding the head from which all the body by joints and bands having nourishment ministered and knit together increases with the increase of GOD. I read to learn about my LORD. I will increase my understanding (Col. 2:19v.).

"Fear none of those things which you shalt suffer: behold, the devil shall cast some of you into prison, that you may be tried; and you shall have tribulation ten days: be you faithful unto death, and I will give you a crown of life. Him that overcome" (Rev. 2:10v.). Be strong in the LORD.

Oh children, fear GOD! This is the last time. Remember the pillar set up on the right called Jachin and the left called Boaz (to the wise). O children of GOD wisdom is the beginning of knowledge, knowledge of the Holy is understanding. All GOD'S children need to read, you will never understand this is the last time.

Revelation: Church of Laodiceans

Seventh Church: Laodicea!

Revelation 3:14-20v.: "These things I write to the city of Laodiceans [all the masons]; These things said, LORD GOD, the amen the faithful and true witness, the beginning of the creation of the GRAND FATHER GOD; I read about you and thy works that my LORD GOD wrote (to the wise), that you are neither cold nor hot: Our LORD GOD would you wert cold nor hot. My FATHER LORD GOD JESUS CHRIST ALMIGHTY will not forget, he sworn by the excellency of Jacob and will not forget any of your work!" (See Amos 8:7v.).

So then because you are lukewarm and neither cold nor hot, my LORD GOD will spew you out of my mouth. Ha!

I will show you that all the things you have are nothing. You say, "I am rich and increased with goods and have need of nothing." You do not know you are wretched, miserable, poor, blind, and naked. What vow have you made unto my LORD GOD? No one can tell the one who knows everything anything.

My LORD GOD counsels you to buy of the LORD gold tried in the fire, so you may be rich, and white raiment, so you may be clothed and the shame of your nakedness will not appear. Anoint your eyes with eye salve so you may see. I, Andrew Jesses Scales, say to everyone, "Read for yourself". No one will tell the one that knows everything; anything.

As many as my LORD GOD loves I will also rebuke and chasten. Be zealous, therefore, and repent. I will rebuke you with my LORD'S Word unless you try to put your hands on me. But my LORD will do more. Repent!

I write this to the wise: Behold, I stand at the door and knock. If any man hears my voice and opens the door, I will come in to him and sup with him and he with me. Do you believe that your riches will get you where you need to go? Repent! Yeah! I set to my seal that the time is at hand. I write to all, repent.

What JESUS Knows!
I Am that I Am! Look Up.

To the children in Laodicea, as I wrote to the other cities.

My FATHER is the Alpha and Omega, the first and the last, and what I read, I write in a book. I will publish it and send it unto the seven churches that are in Asia: unto Ephesus, and unto Smyrna, and unto Pergamos, and unto Thyatira, and unto Sardis, and unto Philadelphia, and unto Laodicea.

"For by fire and by his sword will I, in the name for the LORD plead with all flesh: and slain of the LORD shall be many" (Isa 65:16v.). My LORD GOD will show you better than we can read!

John will have to prophesy again. Have you read this in the Revelation? This is me from JESUS CHRIST, who is the faithful witness, the first begotten of the dead, and the prince of the kings of the earth. He loved us and washed us from our sins in His own blood. I will be his son, are you?

"And John saw heaven opened, and behold a white horse; and he that sat upon him was called Faithful and True, and in righteousness he doth judge and make war. I am that I am. I am send me to tell all the children, I am the son of CHRIST" (Rev. 19:11v.). We are his sons and daughters.

I wrote to the city in Philadelphia also, "These things saith he that is holy, he that is true, he that hath the key of David, he that openeth, and no man shutteth; and shutteth, and no man openeth" (Rev. 3:7v.).

Who is he who sat on the white horse? He who sat upon him was called Faithful and True, and in righteousness he judges and makes war. Have you read in Revelation that there are two men?

I, Andrew Jesse Scales, will answer as my FATHER JESUS answered and said unto them, "Though I bear record of myself, yet my record is true: for I know whence I came, and whither I go; but you cannot tell whence I come, and whither I go. Amen" (John 8:14v.).

Understanding Finds Knowledge!

"What is the mystery, which from the beginning of the world hath been hid in GOD, who created all things by JESUS CHRIST" (Eph. 3:9v.). Who is the image of the invisible GOD, the firstborn of every creature?

Oh children, it is written, "Ephraim said, Yet I am become rich, I found me out substance in all my labors they shall find none iniquity in me that were sin. All the money in the world will not get you where you need to go."

Laodiceans, now you are full, now you are rich, and you have reigned as kings without us. I would to GOD you did reign so we also might reign with you (1 Cor. 4:8v.).

One day I will say, "Yea, Ho, every one that thirsteth, come you to the waters, and he that hath no money; come you, buy and eat: yea, come, buy wine and milk without money and without price" (Isa. 55:1v.).

"O children, the kingdom of heaven is like unto treasure hid in a field; which when a man hath found, he hideth, and for joy there of goth and selleth all that he hath, and buyeth that field. I found the treasure; I will not hid" (Matt. 13:44v.).

Oh children, do you understand? "They are all plain to him that understandeth, and right to them that find knowledge" (Prov. 8:9v.). I will make it plain. When you read for yourself, you will find you have the field and it is paid for.

These words are to you that have wisdom: "You have a few names even in Sardis which have not defiled their garments; and they shall walk with me in white: for they are worthy" (Rev. 3:4v.).

Love and Keep My Words!

It is written unto me and all my brothers and sisters, "My sons and daughters, despise not the chastening of the LORD; neither be weary of his correction" (Prov. 3:11v.).

I will covet earnestly the best gifts, and yet I show you a more excellent way. Read for yourself the LORD'S Word (1 Cor 12:31v.).

I write to all the world. Remember, therefore, how you have received and heard and hold fast and repent. If you will not watch, our FATHER LORD GOD JESUS CHRIST ALMIGHTY will come on you as a thief and you will not know what hour JESUS will come upon you.

"And you yourselves like unto men that wait for their LORD, when he will return from the wedding; that when he cometh and knocketh, they may open unto him immediately" (Luke 12:36v.). I also wait, and I know when He is coming back.

"JESUS answered and said unto him, If a man love me, he will keep my words: and my FATHER will love him, and make our abode with him. He that endure." (John 14:23v.). I know JESUS is the truth, and JESUS is love.

I thank the only FATHER and only LORD GOD JESUS!

I hope to hear from you soon and see you. JESUS is love.

Thank you,
Andrew Jesse Scales

PS: These things I write are to all my brothers and sisters of every kinder, tongue, people, and nation. This is the last time!

In JESUS's name I thank our GRAND FATHER. (I must endure.)

"We shall know the truth, and the truth shall make us free!" (John 8:32v.).

I read, write, and send what you see to the seven churches. I, in the name of my FATHER LORD GOD JESUS CHRIST ALMIGHTY, thank my only GRAND FATHER. I read and run so you may obtain the prize (1 Cor 9:24v.). I know the truth will make us free. I read that there is a LORD, and there is no GOD besides Him (Isa. 11:17v.). I know and believe that the LORD GOD is JESUS CHRIST ALMIGHTY. I read what my LORD delights in (Jer 9:24v.). I have read, and reading the LORD GOD'S Word is for our learning. We will learn patience, and reading the Scriptures will give us hope (Rom. 15:4v.). I also read, "Let everything be done for edification." I know by reading that the testimony of JESUS CHRIST is the spirit of prophecy (Rev. 19:10v.). And for all who believe in JESUS CHRIST, there is no difference. I believe there is an end, and our expectation will not be cut off (Prov. 23:17v.). In the latter days I read: you will consider it perfectly. This book that I share with you is for all the LORD GOD'S children of every kinder, tongue, and nation. This is the last time.

Now we know that our expectation is of what is ALMIGHTY. For edification we read that JESUS CHRIST is LORD GOD ALMIGHTY. We know by reading that the Revelation is what will take place. We also know the Revelation shows us that JESUS has a son who belongs to one of the seven churches. What is your expectation? And where is CHRIST's son? (See Rev. 21:7v.). If you read, see also 1 Corinthians 10:26v., 9:26, and 9:24v. It will show us that we all run in the race for a prize that the LORD GOD will give each of us. Remember. you stand alone! Who will tell the one who knows everything anything? I write what I see. I do not run uncertainly. I fight I with the faith I have in my LORD GOD. I thank my GRAND FATHER. Oh GRAND FATHER, I know all is the LORD GOD who will show us better than we can read. I write out of the gospel to share with my brothers and sisters knowledge of the holy and to give them understanding, for necessity is laid upon me. Yea! Woe unto me if I do not write (1 Cor 9:16v.). I know the LORD GOD will recompense or requite us. Oh children, will the LORD GOD bring all our work into judgment, good or bad? Is any secret thing withheld from our LORD GOD (Eccles. 12:14v.)?

What is our duty? The duty of everyone is to fear GOD and keep His commandments (Eccles. 12: 10-14v.). I testify to all that it is a fearful thing to fall in the hands of our LORD GOD (Heb. 10:31v.). Fear of the LORD GOD is the beginning of wisdom, and knowledge of the holy is understanding (Prov. 9:10v.). The days will come when our LORD GOD will put a little wisdom in everyone's heart and mine (already in mine,fearful thing to come in the hand of the LORD). I see them hasty with their words, not knowing there is more hope for a fool than for them (Prov 29:20v.). In vain do they worship GOD, teaching doctrines of the commandments of men (Matt 15:9v.) until we all come in unity of the faith and knowledge of the son of GOD, the fullness of CHRIST. And do not be tricked by those who say they have GOD or this and mean that and that and mean this. Oh nations, I say if I can teach, let me teach you to read for yourself. You stand alone!

Go to: runallgodschildren.com and I will read. You can read also. Come, come, come all. This is the last time!

This book is for edification.

Thank you, children, for reading what has happened and what is going to happen! This is the last time!

Why? The LORD Is So Angry!

"Write to the seven churches that are in Asia." This is why this book is being published. I set to my seal that GOD is true. This book is to share with you. This is the last time. We all read the same Holy Word. We all know that the truth will make us free. I publish this to let everyone know that I am in the race for the prize in the Holy Book.

It is written in John 8:32v., "And you shall know the truth, and the truth shall make you free."

I called on our GRAND FATHER and our FATHER LORD GOD JESUS CHRIST, and I received my testimony to share with you. (And this is the last time.) I received the holy word over thirty years ago, I went to many places, and some told me to get out. I am a mason, and I know who the seven churches are to put a little light on what is happening, and I am a chaplain. I was on the radio for about fifteen years. A man bought the station I worked at. I paid him for my spot, and he just took my money. I only went on two times. I went to the newspaper and showed them my book, but that was nothing. I also paid a US newspaper and said, "I am in the race for the prize in the Holy Book." One man wrote me back who read it in the paper. I went to mason halls and churches, and they took me lightly.

Who believes in the Holy Word? Who believes in the prophets or JESUS CHRIST? If I teach, I would teach you to read for yourself. You stand alone! I have put together what has happened and what is going to happen. Are GOD'S children running in the race for the prize in the Holy Book? Do they know there is a race? Well, I'm running and when I win, I will share the prize with all GOD'S children. Do you know what LORD GOD (JESUS) delights in?

It is written in Jeremiah 9:24v., "But let him that glorieth glory in this, that he understandeth and knoweth me, LORD which exercise loving kindness, judgment, and righteousness, in these things I delight, Saith the LORD."

How to Know the LORD: Read the Revelation of JESUS LORD GOD. This is the end of what He is going to do. I will show you with His word that He (JESUS) is our FATHER.

It is written 2 Corinthians 6:18v., "And will be a FATHER unto you, and you shall be my sons and daughters, saith the LORD ALMIGHTY.And

You can go to runallgodschildren.com and read with me for edification. It is time for the truth.